T0209981

LOVER, FIGHTER, WRITER

POETRY FOR THE AWAKENING WARRIOR

BRIGITTE NARCISE

BALBOA.PRESS

A DIVISION OF HAY HOUSE

Balboa Press books may be ordered through booksellers or by contacting:

Balboa Press
A Division of Hay House
1663 Liberty Drive
Bloomington, IN 47403
www.balboapress.com
1 (877) 407-4847

Because of the dynamic nature of the Internet, any web addresses or links contained in this book may have changed since publication and may no longer be valid. The views expressed in this work are solely those of the author and do not necessarily reflect the views of the publisher, and the publisher hereby disclaims any responsibility for them.

The author of this book does not dispense medical advice or prescribe the use of any technique as a form of treatment for physical, emotional, or medical problems without the advice of a physician, either directly or indirectly. The intent of the author is only to offer information of a general nature to help you in your quest for emotional and spiritual well-being. In the event you use any of the information in this book for yourself, which is your constitutional right, the author and the publisher assume no responsibility for your actions.

Any people depicted in stock imagery provided by Getty Images are models, and such images are being used for illustrative purposes only. Certain stock imagery © Getty Images.

Print information available on the last page.

ISBN: 978-1-9822-4232-9 (sc)
ISBN: 978-1-9822-4233-6 (hc)
ISBN: 978-1-9822-4231-2 (e)

Library of Congress Control Number: 2020901961

Balboa Press rev. date: 02/10/2020

To Donnie, for whom loving, fighting, and writing always seemed to be inextricably intertwined and infused with otherworldly intensity. While she actually wrote the final two poems included here, she certainly inspired many more to come through me, and for that, and for countless other gifts, I am eternally grateful. See you on the other side, Mom. Your voice never fades.

CONTENTS

THE LOVER

THE FIGHTER

THE WRITER

EPILOGUE

THE LOVER

LOVE NOTES FROM THE UNIVERSE

DIVINE FAMILIAR

I had a name for you once;
it seemed to fit,
when I scarcely knew you –
who you were,
what you were.
Unbeknownst to me then,
you had so many names,
you had so many faces.

Chimerical and powerful,
soft and steady, that you were;
I tried these names all so familiar,
but no human calling was complete
in summing up your everything,
with such a common sound or two,
how could that ever, ever do?
in serving to define
your Great All-Energy, and
everything you are to me –
Divine

DREAM A LITTLE DREAM

The dream was real;
my body believed it,
still humming and now
still grasping for you.

Tossed ruthlessly to Earth,
your lips torn from mine,
blood afire like turpentine-
lit and vanished in a flash,
now awake, empty and dazed
but sure I just crossed time and space
with you wrapped around me,
so tell me please –
how could this be
just a dream
just a little, little
little dream?

CONSPIRACY

Make no mistake:
the worlds have conspired
to match each circumstance
of infinite time and space
for us to be together
Now.

FACES OF YOU

Each time I see you,
you are born anew;
never the same view
to me!

Upside down,
I see you now;
looking back at me
so serene,
then giggling –
or sober and stern
from challenging concerns;
not the same face at all
today from yesterday,
and tomorrow what will play
on my eyes,
on my mind,
on my heart?

RIPPLES AND WAVES

Precious, priceless face,
finest art of all;
your voice is my music,
your presence so soothing,
calming and smoothing
the ripples of my soul.

All my worries and
indeed, my existence,
quiet and fade
as I lie ear to cage,
and hear without hearing
all worldly solutions and
secrets for peace
being spelled out in code,
in melodious mode,
by the rhythmic hammering
of your beautiful heart,
making happy new waves
today in my soul.

WE

If only I could fold up your essence,
and tuck you into a suitcase;
indeed, then I would take you
every place.

I could wheel you around,
town to town,
over land and over sea,
you'd go everywhere with me
and I would never be
I or me,
but forever us,
together –
We.

EYE SIGH

Amber amulets hung side by side
are your eyes in bright sunlight,
but in shadows bake
into molten maple syrup
in the sweet stack of your face.

Twin shots of warm cognac,
drunk from your gaze,
spread cozy heat in ardent waves
but in neither darkness nor in light,
your eyes cannot deny
their luminous reflection
of this world's perfection –
I sigh!

SUMMATION

She was everything,
She had everything,
and He was everything
to Her.

All She could ever want,
ever dream to behold,
was Hers thanks to Him –
Him who adored Her.

Him for whom
She gave everything;
He was the treasure,
He treasured everything.
She became everything
to Him.

TWIN SOULS

She was drowning and
his lips brought the first taste of air;
as she breathed in his essence,
nothing compared.
It drove her to claw
and grab for the source
of inebriating vapor
and now drink and savor
more of his feast
that fueled her awake
and alive in 5-D.

She presses, interlopes,
but their skin hateful barriers,
chaining them, barring passage.
She hums from her core,
and a vibrating energy
penetrates through his pores:
they are separate no more.
Recognition floods through,
what was thought to be two,
and decidedly melts that illusion.

WICKED MOON

Wicked moon, glowing full,
always rousing me from slumber!
Willing me to wake and write,
willing me to walk the night –
compelled to rise, and go outside,
as though I hear my Romeo
calling William's verses
from high above my window,
not below,
but I must go –
under the sky, out to greet him,
in his fullness and completeness!
A siren's call heard by my soul,
and for one moment in his glow,
I am sure of all I know
and all is all is all
is well
below.

FORMIDABLE YOU

Who can imagine the You I know?
How incredibly lovely and soft
the silky pink underside is –
the hidden belly of this,
most untouchable beast.

RIVER MEETS SEA

Life-giving water pulses ahead
where River meets Sea,
determined to reach her,
to breach her
estuary.

A trove of gems and silken silt
lay left behind each previous time;
sharp rocks and smooth sand,
the calling card of every man.

His fresh current penetrates,
purposefully moving,
mixing into her boundless depths,
convincing her that
she could be more
than ever before,
and delightfully less salty.

SHHHHHH

In the dark,
I see you better
and hear you so well
in the silence
I know you best,
right here and now –
shhhhhh

SOMETIME EVERYWHERE

Sometime, Everywhere
I loved you.
In the darkness, in the light,
in ancient times and lives to come,
in the shadow of innumerable suns,
I loved you.

Everytime, Somewhere
alone, despaired and blind;
running in an endless night,
separated now from All That Is,
I hold for you the Vision of Bliss
as long as it takes to wake to share,
I loved you, I love you,
Every Time, Every Where.

LOVE WORDS

Love, love, I always write about love...
for can there ever be enough
love words,
expressions, affections;
written, spoken, acted?

Can there ever be enough
or too much
extolled on depths
of passion and longing?

Sentimental affirmation,
agony and elation,
which make us so exquisitely
alive yet converged
with all our selves –
such is love, love, only love.
Let's write about love.

RAVAGED

Not asking permission, he takes –
without second thoughts;
decisive, forceful; kingly, not boyish,
but graces unknown, apologies foreign;
too much to reconcile, to wrap
her narrow perspective around;
now soaked in sorrow and passion,
irreparable, irrepressible,
the heart of the savage.

No invitation, she comes –
a live hurricane
of careless opinion and presence;
demanding, exceeding all or nothing,
high expectations fulfilled, or bludgeoned;
too much to reconcile, to aspire,
from the programmed view he had;
rampant resistance afire,
so cloaked and soaked
in sorrow and passion,
these fine hearts,
ransacked and ravaged.

ACCIDENTAL LOVE

Oh accidental love,
where did you come from?
I was not asking, not expecting,
and certain, so certain
I didn't need you in my life!

Oh accidental love,
don't you always injure someone?
I was safe and content
and now broken and bent,
but these pieces create
the most beautiful of mosaics.

HOMECOMING

He aims to slip inside
like a thief in broad daylight;
his presence at the threshold
respectfully hushed,
but not at all subtle.

Surging and stretching
himself to full height;
aroused, awakened, he sighs,
and with that single breath,
breaches the darkness
and explodes into light.
She screams
in all-encompassing delight!
He has arrived.

LOVE SIMILES

I love you like the moon
loves the dark night sky;
growing ever bigger and brighter,
her illumination
the show of ages.

I love you like the rose
loves the summer sun;
his radiance deepening
her heady fragrance,
not yet to be released.

I love you like the seed
loves the warm spring earth;
cozily resting, gathering unto itself
the Creator's energy,
to burst forth at last.

I love you like I love myself
and hate myself, my childish id;
its flaws and tantrums forgiven,
as we evolve, expand, and love;
my forever, eternal love.

OUTCOMES

So outrageous sometimes
the things you say, like
"What if we had never met?"
as though that could have ever been
an outcome of this master plan;
as if the earth were flat,
or dragons were real,
or that I could stop myself
from thoughts of you
pouncing unbidden through my psyche
when asleep and awake,
relentless in my head,
and for certain it continues
long after I am dead.
So how could we have never met
when I know you live
inside of me?

BEFORE WORDS

A thousand hours spent
near each other but apart;
in blessed silence side by side,
with so few muddled words
uttered or heard;
for so many years in motion
with just gestures and expressions,
laced in simple, deep perceptions.

And although we seemed unknown
to each other's human forms,
we were hopelessly entangled
already for so long;
and such content and ease we felt
for all those early days,
until we started speaking
and the words got in the way.

VANISH

Let me drown in your essence;
plunge into that endlessly deep,
rolling river current!
Icy cold, every cell of my being tingles
and I hear, feel, and sense nothing else
except the oneness of you
enveloping my skin, my scent, my breath;
transforming me,
making the me I knew
vanish.

NOW

Make no mistake,
the worlds have conspired
to match each circumstance
of infinite time and space
for us to be together
now.

X-TOWN

My love whispers of a land
where lush, verdant mountains
touch the clouds with cold hands;
all the while, grassy feet
stick tip-toes in the sea –
Such a place, could there be?

The name rolls from his tongue,
strange sounds like singing bees
that mean nothing to me;
in a moment irretrievable,
yet this sounds unbelievable!

My mind is not convinced
this earthly place does exist,
where hills dance in salt mist;
a sandy blackness of sea,
wrapped in vivacious green
embraces like we,
and like X-town,
no one remembers our name.

I BELONG TO YOU

If I should die before my time,
let your lips meet mine,
and Anubis will recognize
that I belong to you.

A whisper, sweet breath,
and we can cheat Death!
Grab my hand, palm to palm,
lines of life pressed together;
squeeze with your passion,
and love beyond measure,
and though we may not stay
on Earth here forever,
the gods will know –
(they will know)
they are never to sever
twin spirits enjoined
in a marriage divine,
and Anubis will recognize
that now and for all of time,
I belong to you.

THE FIGHTER

THE HUMAN EXPERIENCE

CHAMPION

In your quest
to win the fight,
you are not very nice,
Champion.
Winning at all costs,
perhaps not as satisfying
as you'd thought.

For truly,
who reigns as victor
when one concedes to silence
just to end all the bicker?

Resentment still festers
and rips holes in our
nascent Resolution,
savagely slaying
the blessed babe;
a magical creature
we've never seen,
only dreamed of –
and prayed.

But savor your triumph,
as he bleeds on the floor,
for you are so deserving –
you wanted it more.

TANGLED

Her beautiful smooth surface
gave no hint of the complexity beneath;
tangled wires in intricate connections,
woven deep around and under,
twisted at times, so hopelessly nonsensical,
the most experienced professional
naught dare to give a price in time
of what it might take to put her right,
and remap this odd and twisted mess,
to make her flow and whole again.

THE FIGHT BEFORE
THE FIGHT

Such faith we have
in this body to heal!
Demanding recovery
from wretched abuse
in our quest to test
all limits of blessed corporeal.

Eyes dry and lips crack,
the heart begins to bang and thrash,
begging for escape from
this depleted trap
of drought and famine (self-inflicted),
to be in near-death moments lifted,
and then ensues a buxom climax
most complete with feast and sleep –

Only to wake to the day of war
to be physically tested yet once more,
and to suffer, recover,
and do it all over again!

RED

Red, she was,
inside and out;
fiery blood so intense,
it could melt iron
to a malleable mess.

Red, she was,
to the ends of her hair,
the length of each nail;
at times, even her eyes
flashed crimson
like full red moons
against the ominous sky
of her similarly dark soul.

Red, she was,
unpainted probing lips,
sanguine and solar-kissed;
red skin so radiant that
the deeper you probed,
the hotter her core.

Red, she was,
with saber-toothed aura;
larger than life, this inferno-cat
consumed any room;
a bubbling vortex, her physical form,
queen of this storm,
a pyro-tigress of a girl,
she was
Red.

DIKAR

(The Noble Savage)

This day of all days,
I met a noble savage.
He was a warrior I guess,
judging from his dress
and formidable demeanor,
quite intimidating, yes!
His visage, grim at best,
but when at last he spoke,
in most calm and measured tones,
I was impressed but taken back,
still suspecting an attack,
unsure if I could trust the beast -
How noble was this savage?

He said he saw for sure in me
this same inherent savagery -
Athletic prowess yet unbidden,
buried deep but not quite hidden
from him as deft and knowing
of beastly spirits locked within.

His sacred quest was now to find
those rare among us,
or not quite,
with lurking lion locked inside,
within their flesh façade of human normalcy
- this beast!

Born and bred of honor code
with every fiber, it was sewn,
each drop of blood and every cell,
knew the code and knew it well;
to teach such things
is not to tell
with complex words or pointless talk,
this beastly king just walked the walk!

I watched and begged my soul to fall
in step, to mimic such as best,
this blossoming of all the rest –
of loyalty and honor pledged
beyond the bonds of ancient kin –
of all our savage brothers.

I was initially not thrilled
with his idea of savage training;
this was suffering and straining,
so absurd and strange to me,
my human form objected loudly!
But he ordered and cajoled
the sleeping lion to the fore,
and soon my human was no more;
the savage self, unleashed at last
but what of me, what of me?

My old life no longer fit;
I was too far gone to quit
this chimeric transformation,
expert now in pain infliction,
now a wicked dereliction –
getting pleasure from the pain
I sought to give.

Resistance broken,
I was pledged
warrior-lion, perfect blend;
this day of all days
I became
a noble savage.

BOXES

Why must I check a box?
Please, yes, check a box!
For our political convenience,
it's so much easier
when things are labeled
white or black or Asian!
– Except I am not a box!
But an amalgamation
of all things human,
of all things worldly,
– and not.

Seemingly female
but perhaps today,
acting more male;
seemingly white
but perhaps inside,
colored more brown.
Anger abounds
while drawing lines
for gender and race,
creating economic, ethnic
and cultural borders,
espousing these differences,
tossing away all
that we truly are,
bound by all
of our similarities and differences.

Can we peel off
this toxic plastic wrapper
of societal pressures,
of political agendas and media frenetics
who print a label that screams
their version of us
so neatly described and designed,
so fancy and pretty…succinct?!
I will not be packaged, not be
someone's object to protest
for or against
to vilify, to glorify…not I!
I am so much more than that!
I am all those things,
all those categories,
all those boxes,
- and none.

For I,
I am me
I am you
I am us
I am not
a box.

LESSER ME

Can you not occasionally accept
the lesser version of me –
the struggling, human version of me;
the damaged, animal version of me?

And I will be grateful and accept
the lesser version of thee;
and patiently but constantly
hold tight in my eyes and heart and head
the finest version of you,
instead?

THE MATRIARCH

The matriarch was yesterday's child,
who ceremoniously shed
her cousins' hand-me-down clothes
for fine shoes and cashmere,
and buried those cousins
one at a time,
year after year,
after burying grandparents,
and uncles and aunts,
and Mother at last;
although Father lived on,
his mind was far gone,
leaving her to grasp to cling,
anticipating desperately,
further loss of fading tribe
and her the nearly next in line.

Yesterday's child adored flowers
but that odor of funerary now
makes the matriarch sick.

THE PATH

In the center of the street,
I move my feet;
rapidly, smiling,
eyes shut
yet I move quickly –
confidently, I strut.

No matter
I can't see as I stride,
for I can feel the path inside.
I caught a glimpse
only once;
just a flash
of the path
before me,
– it's enough.

Can't you see?
A glimpse is
all you need
to stride ahead,
and when you halt
and pause to breathe,
you'll be precisely where
you dreamed you'd be.

ADAM

Wicked lips that curse or kiss,
ragged nail on a fingertip,
steep chin and dimple within,
sharp angles of a jaw that flex
to corded muscles in the neck,
cradling the fruit forbidden –
rocked to sleep
when he speaks,
this divine treat,
shared after Eve took her bite,
freeing them both,
he carries it always,
suspended in the space
between heart and mind,
the telltale sign
they are two of a kind,
and reminder of whence
they had came.

SILLY FLESH WOUNDS

She was certainly, irrefutably
changed for having known him;
scars peppered her face,
crossing this way and that;
a tear duct split and stitched,
even crying was never the same.
Her nose had gained character
since they'd met,
so typically, boringly Roman
it had been.

Cracked and twisted wrist and toes;
concussions, fractured facial bones,
lips split and eyebrows glued,
so much fun they had
testing these limits,
gaping in wonder at
their superpowers to heal
these silly flesh wounds.

STUPID DRUNK

If you tried to hurt yourself
in some old-fashioned way,
other than to drink to take
your life and love away;
if you ingested arsenic,
instead of wine and beer,
could we have managed then
to fully interfere?

Could we have made a scene,
and locked you safe away?
Safe and angry and unhappy,
to live until today?
A victim of addiction,
of attempted suicide;
victim of a broken system,
mental problems so maligned.

Freedom treasured,
courts approved,
deliver liquor, paltry food;
drunk and starving tiny waif,
bleeding out and never bathed;
desperate, filthy -
ambulance;
catch and free,
it never ends.

Relentless, vicious alcohol!
Your mind and body, even soul,
no longer yours to wield control;
such like every wretched crime -
pain slowly festering in kind,
and rots you from the core inside -
a dank, molasses suicide.

Alcohol, drop by drip,
hateful now, I feel you slip;
and I am clearly not enough
for you to quit and give it up.
If it was poison-pure indeed,
could someone then have intervened?
And we could dream –
(oh, could we dream?)
that things had worked out
differently.

THE FIGHTER

In the walk of ages, he is
a Gladiator,
sequestered in the sub terrain;
pacing the pen, end to end,
focused and silent,
they wrap his hands,
hardened fists,
most precious and treasured,
to flow in perfect
pain-inflicting concert,
with the whole of his being
in measure.

Rules spoken and agreed, he is
an Apache,
riding out on the wave of his tribe;
blood brothers, side by side,
with whispers of honor and fire,
they paint his face,
bless his weapons and part ways
as he explodes into the cage,
this sacred space,
the only place
he is he-
Free.

DIADEM

No matter the time or location,
venture or occasion,
he wears a crown always now;
it never slips and perpetually shines,
weightless as iron and solid as time,
with a sole adornment gracing the brow –
a luminous lemniscate in ceaseless chase
of closing the gap in the ultimate race
to meet – or beat – Her Majesty,
Infinity.

He wears a crown always now;
the diadem a part of him,
as the calcified sabre of the mythical stallion
transforms the horse to a magical beast,
much as he can no longer be
called an ordinary man indeed.

MASTER

You are stronger but
you can't shake me;
you can yell but
you can't make me;
you can smash but
you can't break me;
you can go but
you can't take me –
for I am the only
master of my chains.

SOME WHATEVER

Here I sit
on top of my world,
not a broken, pathetic girl
crying over some whatever,
or a man who
lost his temper,
saying cruel things
to hurt, or worse –
to see myself
as something less
than the divine
feminine,
or commingled
yang to yin,
for am I not
a part of him,
himself, repackaged,
in prettier skin?

PAST LIVES

Once we were trees,
you and I –
fruit bearers with ever-changing
possibilities for growth.

Blossoms bursting,
coloring, perfuming,
creating, producing,
stretching, reaching.
Trees once more.

Once we were lions,
you and I –
ferocious twins with ever-changing
pride and purpose.

Rubbing faces,
sleeping, snuggling,
coupling, sunning,
exploring, hunting.
Lions once more.

Once we were warriors
you and I –
Thracian gladiators in ever-changing
battles of darkness and might.

Shoulders pressing,
swinging, thrusting,
bleeding, twisting,
healing, breathing.
Warriors once more.

Once we were Source
you and I –
paired spirits in ever-changing
visions of flickering light.

Chakras entwined,
floating, flying,
experiencing, vibrating,
transcending, evolving.
Source evermore.

LOST

There is nothing to say,
just an impulse one day
to paint my face
a ceremonial way;
streaks and fat lines
in red, yellow, black.
I trekked a path alone
until its end, and sat
and slashed
and watched the juice of life
leak from me;
splashing on to fallen leaves
colored now anew –
released in a moment,
released from the torment,
I swooned and sighed,
and flew.

JUST A GIRL

I am
just a girl;
a goddess, creator,
a creature, a maker,
a beast and a savior,
a coward, risk-taker,
a healer, ball-breaker,
a timekeeper, a sleeper,
a heathen, believer,
a doll, a witch,
a scratch, an itch,
a tyrant, a slave,
a mansion, a cave,
eyes brown, eyes green,
a wretched waif,
a perfect queen,
I am, I am
just
a
girl.

BEAST

Before you let me know you,
I already knew you.
I knew who you really were,
while you were still playing pretend games
in a very real fortress
of cultural mores and steel beams of shame,
protecting the good citizens
from witnessing the unthinkable –
a nurturing beast,
yet to be unleashed,
in all his femininity.

The crowds do cower,
but not I –
I dry
your tears.

THE BOY AND THE DOOR

She knew this boy
would walk with angels
and slay dragons,
or befriend them,
as wisdom suggested;
and winged feet would carry him
to stand before the Great Locked Door.

When the Graces deemed it time,
he arrived and stood alone one day;
the Great Door loomed there silently,
its peak reaching into violet sky -
grand and intimidating, it was
rigged with iron hinges, chains
and padlocks two feet thick,
bragging loudly of its dominance
through its myriad of battle scars
left by earlier crusaders;
defeated and exhausted,
they had fallen at the Door.

They had burned and battered,
pounded and pried,
at the Door, at the locks
with their tools and their might,
and the Door held,
as it had always held

secrets of time and space,
secrets to the code of soul and
where the seat of consciousness lays.

She knew this boy,
as wisdom suggested,
would regard this
ominous ogre of a Door,
draped in chains and iron locks
and ever-so-gently turn the knob.

This boy would pull with all he's got –
straight back he'd coax
his hand towards heart;
he knew this Door was never locked,
but who was he to tell them
that the locks were but a farce?
And that pushing against
never gets you what you want.

She knew this boy
with winged feet
would walk with angels
and befriend dragons,
as wisdom suggested,
knowing that the Door awaits
a simple turn and tug to open.

THE HEROINE

"All things come to an end,"
he said;
"Often with the demise
of the headstrong heroine."

She leaves behind:
the story undone –
a trove of amorous prose;
a lover, a son, most treasured
in truth,
some thought her crazy,
most thought her fun,
but none ever thought
that she would die young;
she always just had one more
last thing to say.

THE WRITER

TRANSITIONS

EARTHBOUND FOR NOW

This energy of mine,
it speaks of light divine;
of endless bounds,
loving all and both
the familiar and unknown.

Not separate but enjoined
in desperate silence of the mind,
my love is infused with all
that you have made me.

My spirit travels;
a renegade, a hanged man,
touching rounded corners,
sailing, swimming, flying;
I am resigned
to keep creating –
Earthbound for now.

THE CREATRESS

Her hand flutters,
and waves crest and tumble -
their mist rising and falling,
as rain brings the colors of life,
and love soaks his surface.

Her lips part,
and wind streams forth -
cascading and swirling,
a tornado of motion;
pure energy, focused and wild at once,
whips across his surface.

Her eyes blaze
through his mountains,
onyx canyons, obsidian seas
violated at once
by her penetrating light,
an inferno diffused, now radiant,
cradles and warms his surface.

Her voice sings;
as birds and beasts
add their sounds to the rhythm of him,
he spins and rejoices;
life abounds
on this, this playground -
his surface.

ASLEEP AWAKE

Sleepy boy, silly girl!
Close your eyes, release your mind,
breathe deep the sweet earth air.
Lay your bones, head and hair
to rest awhile, and smile
with your dream-lips, press a kiss
from your soul, awakened.
Good night and hello, my love!
How I've missed you.

TRYST

Fervid water sluiced his Adonic frame,
lasciviously lathered in fragrant foam;
so recently rubbed with the delicious,
salacious musk of her.

Now so resolutely scrubbed and rinsed,
this redolent evidence of their tryst,
released from his skin, intermingled
forever these cells, scents and juices
swirl and dilute to unfailingly end up
again and again,
down the drain.

FOR THE RIDE

She is on the move again,
changing, chasing
a grander version of herself;
so sorry she didn't warn you first
about her super-charged soul
having total control,
but she was yet unaware
that her fleshy existence,
so cared for and prized,
was simply a vehicle
employed for the ride.

MY FINAL SLEEP

Much as I am a fire child,
no fire for me, please,
for my final sleep –
to dream the dream that never ends,
to make the trip to see old friends,
to have and to hold in soothing comfort,
a silent adoration everlasting.

For my final sleep,
this lovely flesh will rest;
this formidable grand palace
was the home for my soul.
It was perfectly built and tended to
for so many years;
I loved this home.
Sometimes I even cleaned up
and invited you to visit in me;
too few minutes you'd stay,
(if you could even enter at all)
then retreat back to your own
soul's home for a sleep.

But always the better were we,
for those moments our spirits played
under one roof –
too bad we couldn't stay!
Alas, this home was all I truly had;
the only thing that was mine alone,
but you always did treasure it so

I would give it when I'm done,
except, I fear it's beyond repair;
and so when I go, it must retreat
for one final sleep
in the earth amongst rocks and trees
to vibrate with my memory,
and return to the Great All-Energy,
until my grander palace gets built
and I shall invite you again.

THAT SKIN

I see you
wrapped inside that skin;
trapped from within
that form that you scorn,
wishing to be seen as more,
to feel intrinsically adored,
as you have always been before,
as you have been evermore -
before you grew that skin.

CLOUDY ENTANGLEMENT

The wind blew clouds
across the blue.
Floating joyously, carelessly,
entangling with another
here and there,
reshaping and birthing
animal faces and figures in white,
then pulling away, yet
taking some, giving some
of what they were;
unconscious floating drifters now,
these clouds,
until they entangle again
with one another.

FOR AVA

Will you catch me
when I'm old and tired and I've had enough,
my roots no longer married to the earth,
but loosening more with every storm?

Will you catch me
when I'm ready to fly, ready to fall,
to give in, give up and jump off
from this turn of the wheel?
To lay down on the fragrant ground
until I become as one with the soil?

When the cold wind blasts
and I tremble and sway,
will you, will you,
will you catch me?

THE TREASURE

She protected her addiction like a treasure;
worthless though it was,
it came to define her.
It permeated every conscious thought
and restlessly pricked and prodded,
even during dreamless slumbers.

It was the handsome rogue who hijacked
every car, plane, train, wagon or donkey
that could take her out of this black town.
God knows she just couldn't manage on foot.
Somewhere along the way,
the rogue had even taken her shoes –
her beautiful expensive red shoes!
Now what was she to do?

Carrying the heavy treasure
was just too much to bear anymore.
It must be hidden, buried,
while she rested like so many times before.
She could lie down beside it
and perhaps the rains and winds
wouldn't cause the dirt to cover her
this time.
Or
she could damn the rogue and walk away!
Barefoot though she was...carless, assless,
her own power maybe was enough –
it had always been enough;
she didn't need that treasure anyway.
She was a queen already.

THAT PLACE

Some place away from my place
is a place unseen, undreamed;
and yet, without a doubt
I know you are there
anchoring that space,
that magical place;
resolutely keeping house
and planting gardens
here and there,
blooms and tombs everywhere;
monuments to buried lives, where
bad choices and transgressions
come to lie and be rinsed clean
by silver tears of rain,
before we come to meet you,
to greet you in that place,
that beautiful place,
where I can always see you.

YES!

She was offered this –
so fragrant and juicy,
so plump with potential
for sweetness and fullness,
completeness and just, well,
adventure!
The possibilities were endless.

Not yet ripe, but the becoming
would be glorious and fun,
and joyful and crazy and happy
and just, well,
exciting –
the growth unfathomable!

So up and down and wild,
so delightful in the
touching, tasting, smelling, seeing
each layer peeled and exalted;
so intense and delicious
it would be,
so she
said "Yes!"

ROUND TRIP

"All things come to an end"
she said, with certainty;
wondering how and when
the story would send her
over the bend and
amend her very self and
turn her outside in.

The hour was growing late and
there was still so much to do,
so much to see,
so much to become,
before coming undone
and returning once more
to the beginning.

PURPOSE

Liking what I do,
ungrateful never,
but true love lost
to some other purpose.

Latent passion,
my unique proposition,
where art thou that sets my blood afire,
and easily pours out
like torrid, fluent lava?

Effortlessly hot, racing downhill
naturally with gravity;
no plan, no choice,
until it cools
and becomes something else
entirely.

MARIGOLD MEMORIES

She thought she caught
the sultry summer scent
of yellow-orange marigolds;
and truth be told,
although she was old,
it made her feel like five years old,
and she was home again.

TREES

Waving green, it breathes
endless purification;
cleansing, healing respiration;
a gift to stave our looming,
dooming decrepitation.
Can't we just give thanks
and treasure these,
our trees?

BUTTERFLY

Don't ask what I can give,
what I can do,
what I wish I could, should,
if choices were mine
this time;
what I am,
what I have,
is a shadow of a hint –
a fleck, a speck,
tiny as a flea,
this existing me,
but oh, what could be
this possible person,
girl to be excavated,
who was once created
already but sleeping;
awoke with a kiss
and another and more;
her cocoon destroyed,
her wings employed –
beautiful, strong, but unsure
they will fly at all.

She stretches and flexes,
a colorful blur –
and is gone.

FROZEN SUNSET

Chasing it down,
westward bound
in a tin bird, so absurd
to relive the past hour
as the sun goes down,
nearly touching the ground,
lighting fire in the clouds
in blazes of orange and red,
as though Heaven itself was burning.

So strange,
it does not fade
within the hour,
and thus my eyes
relay a lie which belies
the message of the fiery
frozen sunset.

Time smiles
and dances around
relative to your here and now,
like the sun only feigning
in touching the ground,
it's just all about where
you are standing.

LATE SPRING

I have been wanting and waiting
and hoping, anticipating,
and dreaming and now
I feel your presence at last!

I was dejected, crushed and confused;
you should have come weeks ago –
before I felt so lost and scared
that the Mother herself
had gone crazy!

BLINK

Soft sounds of live guitar
drift through my bedroom,
waking me to the reality of my here and now;
that the beloved player has suddenly become
a septuagenarian, a white-bearded bard.

The once young father who deftly strummed
through the after-hours of childhood bedtimes
now rises early to play again,
this time in my home, shared with him,
as he shared with me;
the scene and the song so much the same.

The six-year-old girl falls asleep early
to the strumming downstairs
and wakes to the same,
but so much has changed –
She is now forty-eight.

THE CARDINAL AND
THE RAVEN

At some point I traded
the cardinal for the raven,
long before your own spirit
set sail on inky black wings.

Red and black pervasive hues,
since the darkness in the womb –
pierced crimson with the blood of birth,
like red-winged blackbirds caught in flight,
or woodpeckers wild in fading light,
tapping out staccato beats
in a rhythm to their redness;
quieting, eventually, as Evening cloaks
her evanescent black upon their backs.

THE SCRIBE

Just write!
When the moment strikes,
when the Heavens know,
your soul burns aglow,
your hand gives a quiver,
your spine shimmy-shivers;
then comes the command
to put pencil in hand;
a life of its own,
it scribbles away
ridiculous prose,
never seen, never known
to my own thinking cap,
I surmise I have snapped!
Who writes these words?
My self is the scribe,
yet these thoughts are not mine!
Escaping instead
from forgotten lost depths,
they bubble and burst
to my surface at first;
a vibration of mine,
for my hands to transcribe
these words that bring me
such pleasure; I boast -
that my own giddy spirit
must love writing the most!

EPILOGUE

FADE TO LIGHT

SONG OF SHAMROCKS

They jump out and call me
"Look down, look here!"
Mischievous clovers, all overgrown,
interwoven together like emerald-green snow,
each leaf disguising and hiding his brothers.
"Look down, look here!"
- a bodacious four-leaf waves and cries,
catching my eye, and I can't help but spy
the shy and timorous five-leaf
he shaded.

Emboldened now, the young ones do call;
and although I am near,
I pretend not to hear;
petting their patches, I look quite insane,
I have no time for such childish games -
searching for four-leafs,
(the Bigfoot of clovers)
but then, all at once,
their hiding was over!
I saw them suddenly, everywhere!
Dozens at once -
in my toes, in my hair!
I picked them all,
baskets at a time,
and gave them to strangers,
as though they were mine.
Every clover was welcomed
and kept as a sign,

but the magic was borrowed –
not mine, but divine!
And from this truth,
I did convince
friends to gaze down
and ask for a hint
of the glimmer of magic
a four-leaf can give;
and so, at last,
they did!

TAKE ME

Where the mountains meet the sun!
Where the river meets the sea!
There, my love, I am certain,
is the perfect place for me!

MOMMA SAID

Put your ear to the ground;
be aware of the sounds;
when it's time to go,
you will surely know
to hustle up
the buffalo,
and walk a mile
in their moccasins
before you cast
that first stone
from your glass house,
where you hide,
alone inside,
quiet as a mouse,
you dirty louse,
at least you're not
up the creek
without a paddle
this time,
my dear child.

PEOPLE PLEASERS

Please all, please none,
please yourself or come undone;
advice from many,
respect too few,
people pleasers always lose.

MIRROR, MIRROR

Mirror, mirror on the wall,
why do you exist at all?
Reflect my eyes right back at me,
to only guess what they might see;
a glimpse of image won't relay,
the whole of whom I am today.

ONE

I turn to face the sun,
as the flower has done;
yearning, wanting –
are we not the same?
One?

CRAZY, CRAZY, CRAZY

Crazy, crazy, crazy,
in a good way, they say,
like the cat chasing his tail;
joyously spinning, faster and faster,
with no goal but delight
in his dizzying pursuit;
no glorious prize,
nor innards for snacking,
just the fun, fun, fun of attacking!

Crazy, crazy, crazy,
in a good way, they say,
like me for you –
beguilement so dazzling,
with no goal but delight
in repartee and adventures,
from day until night;
no glorious prize,
nor new creature to birth,
(for we pursue only mirth!)
seeking beauty and pleasure
in each dawn new,
cause I'm crazy, crazy,
crazy for you.

BOOTS

If you cannot see the path,
you must feel the path;
but how can you feel anything at all,
when you always have your boots on?

MY FRIEND

She does not speak much
and yet I know she's happy.
She does not eat a lot
and yet I know she's full.

She does not tell me,
but yet I know she loves me.
When I think I am all by myself,
she lies here by me.

Sometime ago we met,
quite by chance at the pound.
She was so lost,
and I was there to comfort her.

So the bond was sewn;
and ever since, our love has grown.
My dog and I are friends;
she need not talk to let me know.

-Written by Donalda Narcise

MOMMY

A tiny, yellow bird
rests gently upon her shoulder.
He sings of love and peace for her;
whispering softly, she asks
the little bird to return.

The soft, yellow bird rests,
waiting patiently;
watching her as she bends and touches
even the tiniest of branches,
covering all the leaves
with a warm blanket of her love.

She waves and beckons the bird to call;
she follows;
the road is lined with the sweet smell
of delicate lavender roses.
Slowly she walks,
kissing each beautiful bloom –
following the little tiny bird,
she finally concludes
her long journey home.

-Written by Donalda Narcise

Printed in the United States
By Bookmasters